EXPLORING COUNTRIES

Kenya

by Jim Bartell

BELLWETHER MEDIA • MINNEAPOLIS, MN

Note to Librarians, Teachers, and Parents:

Blastoff! Readers are carefully developed by literacy experts and combine standards-based content with developmentally appropriate text.

Level 1 provides the most support through repetition of high-frequency words, light text, predictable sentence patterns, and strong visual support.

Level 2 offers early readers a bit more challenge through varied simple sentences, increased text load, and less repetition of high-frequency words.

Level 3 advances early-fluent readers toward fluency through increased text and concept load, less reliance on visuals, longer sentences, and more literary language.

Level 4 builds reading stamina by providing more text per page, increased use of punctuation, greater variation in sentence patterns, and increasingly challenging vocabulary.

Level 5 encourages children to move from "learning to read" to "reading to learn" by providing even more text, varied writing styles, and less familiar topics.

Whichever book is right for your reader, Blastoff! Readers are the perfect books to build confidence and encourage a love of reading that will last a lifetime!

This edition first published in 2011 by Bellwether Media, Inc.

No part of this publication may be reproduced in whole or in part without written permission of the publisher. For information regarding permission, write to Bellwether Media, Inc., Attention: Permissions Department, 5357 Penn Avenue South, Minneapolis, MN 55419.

Library of Congress Cataloging-in-Publication Data
Bartell, Jim.
 Kenya / by Jim Bartell.
  p. cm. – (Exploring countries) (Blastoff! readers)
Includes bibliographical references and index.
 Summary: "Developed by literacy experts for students in grades three through seven, this book introduces young readers to the geography and culture of Kenya"–Provided by publisher.
 ISBN 978-1-60014-576-6 (hardcover : alk. paper)
 1. Kenya–Juvenile literature. I. Title.
 DT433.522.B37 2011
 967.62–dc22   2010039456

Printed in the United States of America, North Mankato, MN.

010111   1176

Contents

Where Is Kenya?

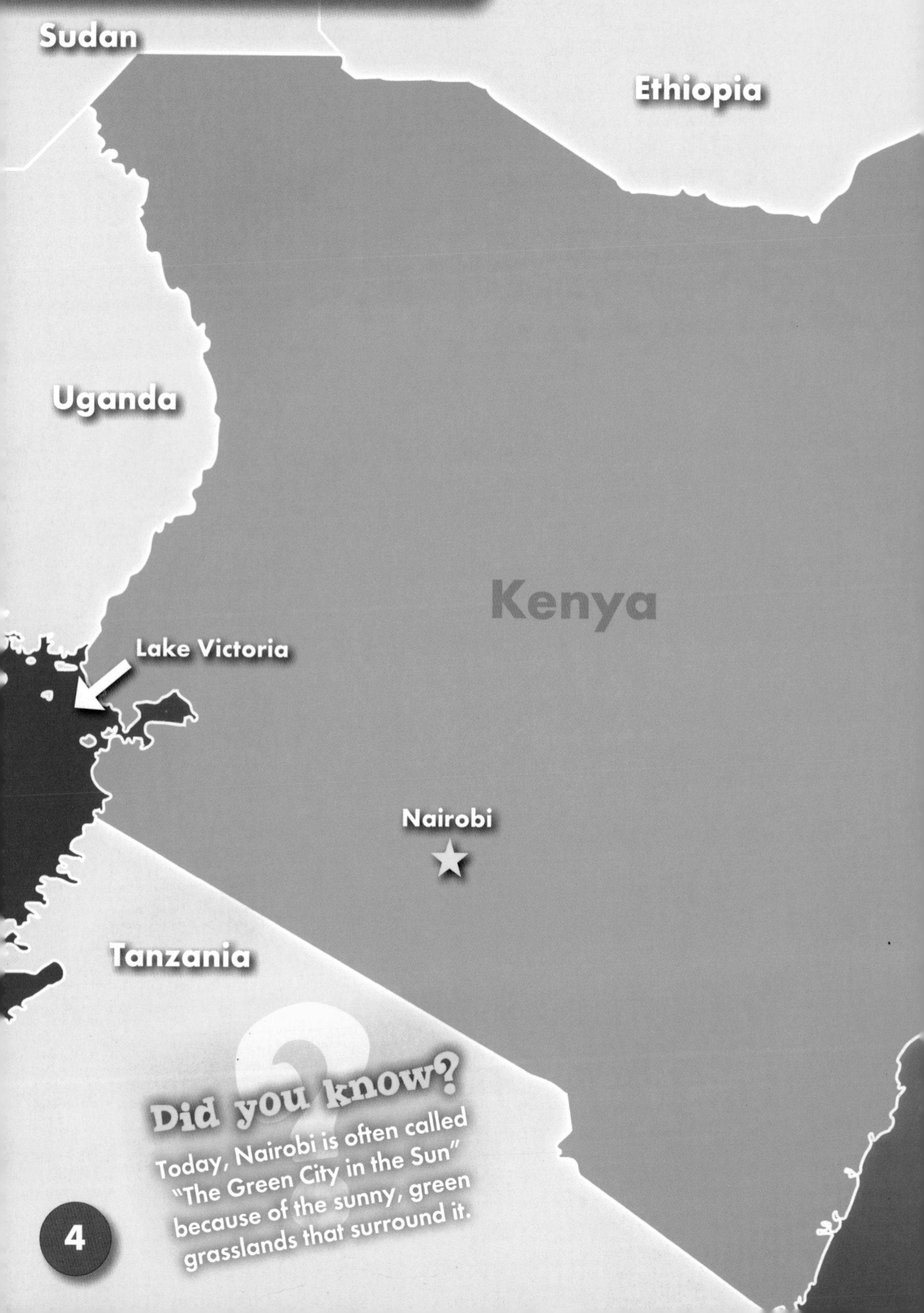

Sudan

Ethiopia

Uganda

Kenya

Lake Victoria

Nairobi

Tanzania

Did you know?

Today, Nairobi is often called "The Green City in the Sun" because of the sunny, green grasslands that surround it.

4

Somalia

Indian Ocean

Kenya is a country in eastern Africa that lies on the **equator**. It is named after Mount Kenya, the second-highest mountain in Africa. The country covers 224,081 square miles (580,367 square kilometers) and is bordered by five other countries. Sudan and Ethiopia touch northern Kenya. To the west sits Uganda, and Somalia and the Indian Ocean lie to the east. Tanzania and Lake Victoria border southwestern Kenya. The capital of Kenya is Nairobi, which means "the place of cool waters."

Great Rift Valley

Mount Kenya

Kenya has mountains, grasslands, and deserts. At 17,058 feet (5,199 meters), Mount Kenya is the highest mountain in the country. It is located in the **Great Rift Valley** in the center of Kenya. Surrounding the mountain is Mount Kenya National Park, which protects the land and wildlife in the area.

In the south, the Serengeti Plain stretches across Kenya's border with Tanzania. Many herds of animals roam this vast plain. Patches of desert are found throughout northern Kenya. In the northwest, the Kakamega Forest spans about 89 square miles (230 square kilometers). This forest is all that remains in Kenya of the **rain forests** that once covered most of Africa.

Did you know?

Kenya's coastline along the Indian Ocean has white, sandy beaches. Out in the water, large coral reefs are home to many kinds of fish and other ocean animals.

Lake Victoria lies in southwestern Kenya on the border with Uganda and Tanzania. It is the largest lake in Africa and the second-largest freshwater lake in the world. The lake is the **source** of the Nile River, which flows north through Uganda, Sudan, and Egypt before emptying into the Mediterranean Sea.

Lake Victoria is important to Kenyans. Its waters hold many kinds of fish that provide food for Kenyans who live near the lake. The lake's beautiful shores and islands also bring visitors from countries around the world.

fun fact

Lake Victoria is named after Queen Victoria, who was Queen of England from 1837 to 1901. English explorer John Hanning Speke, the first European to visit the lake, named it after her.

Did you know?

The Great Migration takes place along Kenya's border with Tanzania. Almost 2 million animals, including zebras, wildebeest, and gazelle, travel in long lines between the two countries.

Kenya has many national parks and nature reserves that protect its unique wildlife. Wildebeest, gazelle, impala, and many other animals roam Kenya's grasslands. Impala can run as fast as 56 miles (90 kilometers) per hour to escape lions and other predators. Cheetahs, however, can run at speeds up to 75 miles (121 kilometers) per hour to catch their prey!

flamingo

hippopotamus

cheetah

Elephants, giraffes, lions, and other animals gather around **watering holes**. They must be careful because large crocodiles and hippopotamuses lurk in the water, ready to strike. Kenya's many lakes are home to fish and large flocks of herons, flamingos, and other birds. Angelfish, butterfly fish, and sea urchins live in the coral reefs off Kenya's eastern coast.

Maasai people

More than 40 million people live in Kenya. Most of them have **ancestors** who were **native** to the lands in and around the country. These Kenyans come from 42 different tribes, including the Kikuyu and the Maasai. Although 3 million people live in Nairobi, only 2 out of every 10 Kenyans live in cities.

Many Kenyans speak English, but almost every native Kenyan speaks a version of Swahili. Each tribe has its own **dialect**. Swahili combines parts of Arabic, German, English, and French. Both English and Swahili are official languages of Kenya.

Speak Swahili!

English	Swahili	How to say it
hello	hujambo	hoo-JOM-boh
good-bye	kwa heri	QUAH heer-ee
yes	ndio	en-DEE-oh
no	sio	SEE-oh
please	tafadhali	TAH-fah-dolly
thank you	asante	ah-SAWN-tee
friend	rafiki	rah-FEE-kee

Most Kenyans live the way their ancestors have for centuries. They work as farmers or herders in Kenya's fields and **pastures**. Homes in the countryside are made of mud and straw. People stay close to their villages, but they travel to markets to trade for food, tools, and other goods. Most of their travel is on foot.

Life is very different in Kenya's cities. Most people live in small city apartments or in houses in the **suburbs**. People use cars, bicycles, and buses to get around. Large outdoor markets bustle with people who buy, sell, and trade goods.

Where People Live in Kenya

cities 22%

countryside 78%

15

Did you know?

Kenya's motto is *harambee*, which means "let us pull together."

In Kenya, children start school at age 6 and must attend until they are 14. They study math, science, and other subjects. Families that can afford it send their children to private schools. Others send their children to public schools. Most Kenyan children, however, attend *harambee* schools. These schools are run by **charities** that provide free food and supplies to the children.

Students take a test when they finish primary school. Their test scores determine where they go to secondary school. Those who complete secondary school can go on to a university. They can study to be doctors, engineers, or teachers.

Where People Work in Kenya

farming 75%

manufacturing and services 25%

Most people in Kenya are farmers. They grow rice, sugarcane, coffee, and tea. Livestock farmers raise cattle, pigs, and **poultry**. Miners also work in the countryside. They dig up limestone, gemstones, and other **minerals**. Factory workers in cities turn these materials into products. In Kenya's lakes and rivers, fishermen catch fish to sell to restaurants and people.

Many Kenyans who live in cities hold **service jobs**. They work in hotels, government offices, restaurants, and banks. Some work in the national parks or at resorts along the Indian Ocean. They show visitors the beautiful landscapes and wildlife of Kenya.

Did you know?
In the 2008 Summer Olympics, Kenya won more medals than any other African country. It took home a total of 14 medals.

Kenyans enjoy many sports and activities. Soccer is the most popular team sport in Kenya. Many people belong to soccer teams in their cities or towns. Track-and-field activities such as running and high-jumping are very popular. Many Kenyan runners compete in races around the world. The best have won medals in the **Olympics**.

In the cities, Kenyans enjoy going to movies and plays. They also like to watch television and listen to music at home. Traditional music and dance are important to many Kenyans. The country's tribes pass special songs and dances down from adults to children.

Did you know?

Bananas and other fruits are popular foods in Kenya. Some Kenyans grow their own, but many buy them from markets.

22

Kenyans eat different foods in different parts of the country. In rural areas, people eat simple dishes made with corn, beans, and meat. Around Lake Victoria and on the coast of the Indian Ocean, Kenyans enjoy many kinds of fish and seafood.

Some dishes, however, are popular throughout all of Kenya. *Ugali*, a mix of corn flour and water, is often eaten with vegetables and *nyama choma*, or roasted meats. *Nyama choma* is usually served with *kachumbari*, a mix of onions, cabbage, tomatoes, and peppers. People boil corn and beans together in a stew to make *githeri*. This dish came from the Kikuyu tribe in central Kenya. A favorite dessert and breakfast food is *mandazi*, or fried dough.

ugali

githeri

Jamhuri Day

Kenya has many national holidays that mark important dates in its history. On December 12, Kenyans celebrate their independence from British rule. Kenyans call this *Jamhuri Day*, or **Republic** Day. They often dress in traditional clothes and listen to the president give a speech. A new **constitution** in 2010 declared October 20 *Mashujaa Day*, or Heroes' Day. This holiday honors important people from Kenya's past, such as Jomo Kenyatta, Kenya's first president.

Kenyans also celebrate many religious holidays. Most people in Kenya are Christians, so they celebrate Christmas and Easter. Many Muslims live along the coast of the Indian Ocean. They celebrate Islamic holidays such as the holy month of **Ramadan**.

lion

Cape buffalo

leopard

When people visit Kenya, they often go on a **safari** to see the country's five most famous animals. These animals are called the "Big Five." They are the lion, Cape buffalo, leopard, rhinoceros, and African elephant. Each animal can be very **elusive** and dangerous. Leopards are able to hide and blend in with their surroundings. Rhinoceroses, Cape buffalo, and African elephants often charge at people who get too close. Lions are strong, fierce fighters with sharp teeth and claws.

In the past, hunters came to Kenya to hunt the Big Five. The horns, tusks, and **hides** of the animals were very valuable. Today, the Big Five represent Kenya's connection to the land. The country's many national parks and wildlife reserves protect these animals, which have become symbols of Kenya to the rest of the world.

Did you know?

European hunters were the first to use the term the "Big Five." They used it to refer to the five African animals that were the most difficult and dangerous to hunt.

rhinoceros

African elephant

Fast Facts About Kenya

Kenya's Flag

The flag of Kenya has three horizontal stripes. The top one is black, the middle one red, and the bottom one green. In the middle of the flag is a traditional Maasai shield and two spears. The flag was adopted in 1963 when Kenya gained its independence from British rule.

Official Name: Republic of Kenya

Area: 224,081 square miles (580,367 square kilometers); Kenya is the 48th largest country in the world.

Capital City:	Nairobi
Important Cities:	Mombasa, Nakuru, Kisumu
Population:	40,046,566 (July 2010)
Official Languages:	English, Swahili
National Holiday:	Republic Day (December 12)
Religions:	Christian (78%), Muslim (10%), Other (12%)
Major Industries:	farming, services
Natural Resources:	limestone, soda ash, salt, gemstones, zinc
Manufactured Products:	food products, clothing, furniture
Farm Products:	coffee, tea, corn, wheat, sugarcane, fruits, vegetables, dairy products, beef, pork, poultry
Unit of Money:	Kenyan shilling

Glossary

ancestors—relatives who lived long ago

charities—groups that collect donations to help people in need

constitution—the basic principles and laws of a nation

dialect—a unique way of speaking a language; dialects are often specific to certain regions of a country.

elusive—difficult to find or catch

equator—an imaginary line around the center of Earth; it divides the planet into a northern half and southern half.

Great Rift Valley—a large canyon that stretches for thousands of miles from eastern Africa to southwestern Asia

hides—the skin and hair of animals

minerals—elements found in nature; salt and zinc are examples of minerals.

native—originally from a specific place

Olympics—international games held every two years; the Olympics alternate between summer sports and winter sports.

pastures—grassy areas where livestock graze

poultry—birds raised for their eggs or meat

rain forests—thick, dense forests that receive a lot of rain

Ramadan—the ninth month of the Islamic calendar; Ramadan is a time when Muslims fast from sunrise to sunset.

republic—a nation governed by elected leaders instead of a monarch

safari—a trip to look at wild animals in their natural habitats; many people who visit Kenya go on a safari.

service jobs—jobs that perform tasks for people or businesses

source—the place where a river begins to flow

suburbs—communities that lie just outside a city

watering holes—places where animals gather to drink water and bathe; watering holes are found throughout the plains of Kenya.

To Learn More

AT THE LIBRARY

Lekuton, Joseph. *Facing the Lion: Growing Up Maasai on the African Savanna.* Washington, D.C.: National Geographic, 2003.

Napoli, Donna Jo. *Mama Miti: Wangari Maathai and the Trees of Kenya.* New York, N.Y.: Simon & Schuster Books for Young Readers, 2010.

Sheen, Barbara. *Foods of Kenya.* Detroit, Mich.: KidHaven Press, 2010.

ON THE WEB

Learning more about Kenya is as easy as 1, 2, 3.

1. Go to www.factsurfer.com.

2. Enter "Kenya" into the search box.

3. Click the "Surf" button and you will see a list of related Web sites.

With factsurfer.com, finding more information is just a click away.

Index

The images in this book are reproduced through the courtesy of: Paul Banton, front cover; Maisei Raman, front cover (flag), p. 28; Jon Eppard, pp. 4-5; Nigel Pavitt / Photolibrary, pp. 6, 6 (small), 8-9, 15, 25; Zute Lightfoot / Impa / Age Fotostock, p. 7; Keith Levit Photography / Photolibrary, pp. 10-11, 12; Foto Factory, p. 11 (top); Ellwood Eppard, pp. 11 (middle and bottom), 23 (left), 26 (top left); Angelo Cavalli / Photolibrary, p. 14; Photoresearch RM / Age Fotostock, pp. 16-17; Eric Isselée, p. 18; Nicholas Pitt / Alamy, p. 19 (left); Charlotte Thege / Photolibrary, p. 19 (right); AFP / Getty Images, pp. 20, 24; Kerstin Layer / Photolibrary, p. 21; Storm Stanley / Photolibrary, p. 22; Mark Skipper, p. 23 (right); David Steele, p. 26 (top right); moodboard RF / Photolibrary, p. 26 (bottom); Johan Swanepoel, p. 27 (top); Johan W. Elzenga, p. 27 (bottom); Emjay Smith, p. 29 (bill); R. Schuster, p. 29 (coin).